My First
Spot the
Difference

Illustrated by Marta Costa Vergili

Written by Elizabeth Golding

Designed by Anton Poitier & Ben Potter

BARRON'S

D1088951

First edition for the United States and Canada published
in 2018 by Barron's Educational Series, Inc.

All inquiries should be addressed to:
Barron's Educational Series, Inc.
250 Wireless Boulevard
Hauppauge, NY 11788
www.barronseduc.com

ISBN: 978-1-4380-1145-5

Date of Manufacture: January 2018
Manufactured by: Grafo SA, Basauri, Spain

Printed in Spain
9 8 7 6 5 4 3 2 1

Get spotting!

This book is jam packed with lots of fun spot the difference puzzles.

There are questions to answer on some of the pages, too!

The puzzles get a little harder toward the end. Don't worry if you get stuck—the solutions are at the back of the book. You'll need to look and look again to find all the differences!

Use a pencil to circle the differences and to write your answers to the questions.

How many differences can you find?

I found ☐ differences.

Find 7 differences between the owls.

Circle each thing that is different.

How many differences can you find?

There are ☐ differences.

These lily pads are different!

I found ☐ differences.

How many differences can you find?

I found ⬚ differences.

Find 4 differences between the planes.

Circle each thing that is different.

Spot the differences!

I found ☐ differences.

How many differences can you find?

I found ⬜ differences.

Circle the differences.

I found ☐ differences.

How many differences are there?

I found ☐ differences.

There are 5 differences. Find them all.

It is a w___y day.

How many differences can you find?

There are ☐ differences.

There are 5 differences. Find them all.

The girl is playing h_psc_tch.

Find 6 differences between these clowns!

Each clown is juggling  balls.

Circle all the differences!

There are differences.

How many differences can you find?

There are ☐ differences.

How many differences can you find?

There are ⬜ differences.

How many differences can you find?

There are ⬚ differences.

Circle all the differences.

There are ☐ differences.

Which knight is ready for battle?

The r_d knight is ready for battle.

Circle all the differences.

I found ☐ differences.

Circle all the differences.

There are ☐ differences.

Find 8 differences between the birthday celebrations!

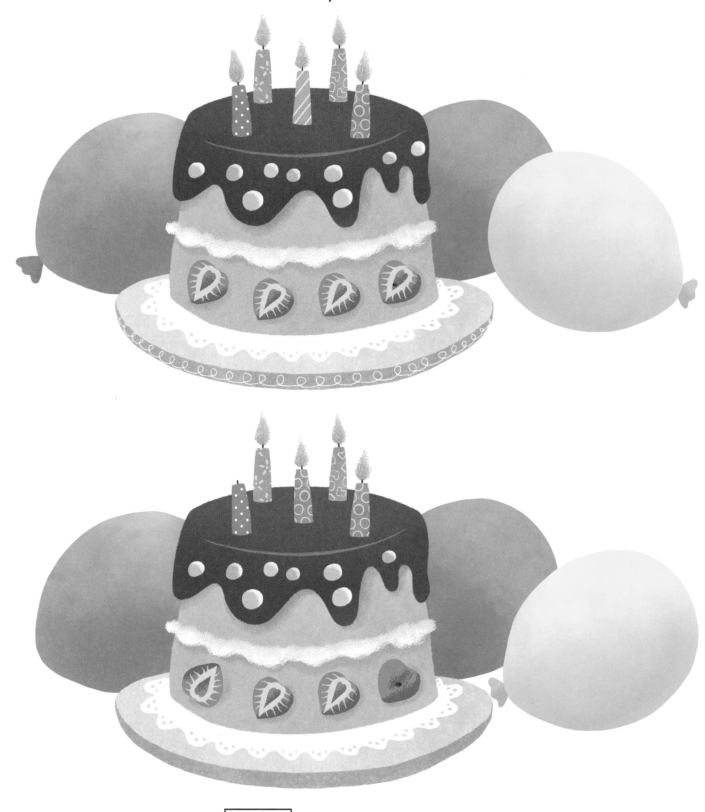

I counted ☐ candles on each cake.

Find 9 differences between the pirates!

The red pirate has only buttons.

How many differences can you find?

I counted ☐ differences.

Find 10 differences between the picnics!

The girl is eating c__e.

How many differences can you find?

I counted ☐ differences.

Find 11 differences.

The crocodile is cooking s_____.

These pictures are different!
Count the differences.

I counted ⬜ differences.

There are 12 differences to find!

How many blue aliens can you see?

How many differences can you find?

I counted ☐ differences.

The cat wants to eat the f__h.

Circle the 13 differences.

The monkeys have long t___s.

There are 13 differences to find.

The dog is chasing a r_ _ _ _t.

How many differences can you find?

I counted differences.

How many differences can you find?

I counted ☐ differences.

How many differences are there?

I counted ☐ differences.

Find 14 differences!

The princess is in the t___r.

Find 14 differences.

How many dogs are in both pictures?

Find 14 differences.

How many stockings are in each picture?

Find 15 differences.

The fox is chasing the c_____s.

Find 15 differences.

The bus driver is wearing a b__e hat.

How many differences can you find?

I counted ☐ differences.

Find 12 differences.

Each castle has flags.

How many differences can you find?

I counted ☐ differences.

Find 13 differences.

Each car has ☐ headlights.

How many differences can you find?

I counted ☐ differences.

How many differences can you find?

I counted ☐ differences.

How many differences can you find?

I counted ☐ differences.

Find 15 differences.

The girl is singing a s__g.

How many differences can you find?

I counted ☐ differences.

Find 16 differences.

The mermaid is sitting on a r__k.

How many differences can you find?

I counted ☐ differences.

Find 18 differences.

The ships are loaded with a c___e.

How many differences can you find?

I counted ⬚ differences.

Find 21 differences.

The experiment is making b_bbl_s.

7

9

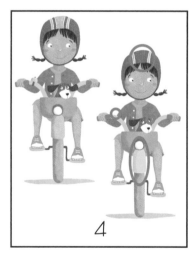

10

4

4

5

5

5

windy

5

hopscotch

5

6

6

6

6

7

red

7

8

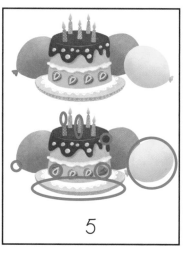

5

2

9

cake

10

sausages

11

2

12

fish

tails

rabbit

13

13

14

tower

2

2

chickens

blue

12

4

13

2

14

14

15

song

16

rock

17

crane

19

bubbles